Fatal Distractions

"The thief cometh not but to kill, and to steal, and to kill, and to destroy. I am come that they might have life, and that they might have it more abundantly." John 10:10

Gretchel Dixon

(GDM Heart2Heart)
ISBN-10: 0692818928
ISBN-13: 978-0692818923

DEDICATION

I would like to dedicate this book to my God-fearing husband, Apostle James T. Dixon. You have been such a blessing to me. You have always encouraged, supported, and pushed me to be all that God has called me to be.

I also want to dedicate this book to my very special gifts from the Lord; my sons J. Christopher Dixon and Jarrod C. Dixon and my three beautiful granddaughters: Briana, Olivia, and Kalyn Dixon. You all are such a tremendous blessing in my life! May God richly bless and prosper you!

CONTENTS

Acknowledgments

Introduction

Introduction Part 2

Forward

ACKNOWLEDGMENTS

I would like to acknowledge all those that have been a part of my life down through the years for your love, prayers, encouraging words, impartations, and support in every way collectively and individually.

Thank you all for believing in the vision that the Lord is allowing me to birth and bring forth to maturity

INTRODUCTION

I am so thankful for Jesus being so real and especially real in my life. As a child, I attended church on a regular basis. Going to church was as common as breathing and going to school. I grew up attending a church that was a traditional denomination. It was not until I went off to college that I discovered that there was more than Methodist, Baptist, and Catholic. I discovered that there were many interpretations of the bible; each person's view influenced the birth of a denomination or as some like to call it" non-denomination". One thing that remains true is "the word of God is the same, today, yesterday, and forevermore". The word of GOD does not change but each person has his or her own interpretation.

I am so thankful that while I had no idea, of whom I was or whose I was; God knew. Jeremiah 1:5 – Before I formed thee in the belly, I knew thee; and before thou camesth forth out of the womb I sanctified thee". What does he mean, "Sanctified"? The dictionary states that it means, "to make holy; set apart as sacred; consecrate; to make productive of or conducive to spiritual blessing. What in the world, does all of that mean? Let us dig a little deeper. Sacred or consecrated means "devoted or dedicated to a deity or to some religious purpose. So now, we have it. Before I was born my parents and grandparents were excited about my upcoming birth, God already knew that I was going to serve him and love him. He also knew about the road I was going to take on my way to fulfilling my purpose.

GOD is so awesome; He does not change his mind about us nor does He give up on us. In fact, He loves us unconditionally. He allowed me to have some distractions along the way that the enemy tried very hard to make fatal. Nevertheless, GOD said not so!

INTRODUCTION PART 2

What is a fatal distraction?

Fatal is defined as (1) causing death; causing failure. Fatal stresses the inevitability of what has in fact resulted in death or destruction.

Let's look at the word fate.

Fate is defined as an inevitable and often adverse outcome, condition or end; (2) the circumstances that befall someone or something.

Distraction is defined as something that makes it difficult to think or pay attention; the act of having thoughts or attention drawn away; the state of drawing thoughts or attention away.

Example: mental confusion-driven to distraction.

Confusion is defined as a situation in which people are uncertain about what to do or are unable to understand something clearly. The feeling that you have when you do not understand what is happening, or what is expected, etc.; a state or situation in which many things are happening in a way that is not controlled or orderly.

FORWARD

My dear godmother, mentor, sister in Christ, and dear friend Apostle, Pastor Gretchel Dixon; words cannot explain the woman you are to me as well as the many others you will continue to reach across the borders.

Pastor Gretchel Dixon is a true woman of integrity. There is so much to say about her, but time and space would not allow me the words to express what an awesome woman she is and has been to me. She entered my family's life as well as mines at a time when we needed it the most. Not knowing the first time, we connected. Over 12 years ago in Austin, Texas would be a life-long God divine connection.

My dear mentor and friend, Apostle Gretchel Dixon not only talks about obedience but her life exemplifies the life of a Proverbs 31 God-fearing woman of God. I know this book "Fatal Distractions" will be a testament of her life and to those that read it shall be blessed.

I want you to, always remember my dear godmother Gretchel Dixon, you were born for this! Even when you think your Goddaughters are not listening, we are. However, "on the other side of the track" of Stephens, AR our inside joke; always remember, "To whom much is given, much is required" as you continue on this victorious journey sharing the Gospel of Jesus Christ and opening doors for others. I am so proud of you as you take it ALL to the next dimension.

I am honored, privileged, and grateful that I am connected with you, as you enter a new season of your life that has been justified and ordained by God. My prayer is that you continue to live a life of no limits! Your best is now!

Love Always,

Apostle Rachel L. Hawkins- Luckett (Your Goddaughter)

When Real Women Pray Ministries

Fatal Distractions

CHAPTER 1

IN THE BEGINNING

It was May of 1952, and my mother Shirley had finally done it; graduated from high school. Her class was the first graduating class of Carver High School. This was a huge accomplishment because several of the students who started elementary school with her dropped out along the way. Some of the students' parents did not feel education was necessary. It was more important to learn how to work in the field and how to take care of farm animals. After all, vegetables were grown to eat and sell; so were cows, chickens, pigs, and goats. However, for my parents, education was very important. Prior to the emancipation proclamation that freed the slaves; African Americans were not allowed to learn to read and write. It has been said that knowledge is power.

My mother grew up in an affluent family but the family struggled because her father squandered his money on other women instead of his wife and three children. The struggle pushed my mother to strive for a better life and a way out of her unhappy home. She was not only smart but beautiful. She knew the only way to change her situation was to change her surroundings. So, she would move in with her uncle and aunt, who lived in a town 20 miles north of her hometown. It was the closest thing to a big city for her. She began to look for work in the small town. During her search for work, she caught the eye of a young cab driver named Robert. My mother had not dated before, which made her an easy prey for the smooth talking Robert. He was the type of man that women liked. He was fair skinned with green and sometimes hazel eyes, had money in his pocket, and a smooth line. He knew what to say and how to say it. I am not saying that he was a devil, but how many of you know that the devil knows what we like and how we like it. The devil will paint such a picture to us as he whispers in our ear to distract us and all the while, we are like a innocent little lamb being led to the slaughter.

9

Soon, after meeting Robert, Shirley and Robert were married. Early into the marriage, Shirley conceived and nine months later, she gave birth to a beautiful baby girl, me, Gretchel.

Unfortunately, for Robert and Shirley, their marriage was very rocky. Robert's inconsistent work schedule driving the cab, inconsistent income, late nights, his flirtatious personality, and the stress of taking care of a wife, a new baby, and his mother, caused him to drink heavily. Robert began to contemplate moving from the Southern United States to the Northern United States. He decided that he and his mother would move to Chicago. He chose Chicago because his mother had two sisters who lived there who offered him a temporary place to live. Shirley refused to follow Robert to Chicago. He wasn't providing the basics of food and shelter for them in a familiar area, so why would she take their baby and leave with him to an unknown area.

You see, Robert had a huge obstacle or should I say many obstacles to overcome. He could not read or write, he stuttered, and he was black. Desegregation had not happened. Racism was still very much alive and well. Shirley chose to move back to her hometown with her parents. She had not heard from Robert for over two years; therefore, she filed for divorce. By the time Robert returned, another man had his wife. Shirley had married a man named Edmond and they were expecting twins.

You see, God just used Robert and Shirley to birth me into the earth realm. God had a much larger purpose. Liken unto Moses, God called me to be a deliver for His people. He allowed me to be raised in the palace (my grandparents' home) and as I grew into an adult, he allowed me to have some wilderness experiences ''Fatal Distractions'' that were meant to kill me but GOD had a plan.

The first 10 years of life with my new father Edmond was good. Then one-day things took a turn. My stepfather was a jealous man. He feared that every man admired his beautiful young wife and at any moment, she would leave him for another man. Edmond was 22 years older than Shirley was. He loved her so much; in fact, he worshiped the ground she walked on. His love for her was greater than the love he ever had for any of his former five wives. She had blessed him with his first child; which turn out to be identical twin boys. Edmond adored his sons. They were a special blessing for him.

 After an afternoon of shopping for shoes for me, my mother and I returned home. Edmond inquired as to where we had been and what we had been doing. I responded by saying, "a man gave mom some shoes". My response incited a huge argument between them. My mother always instructed me to dial the operator and ask for the police if anything happened. As the argument escalated, I went over to dial the operator on our wall-mounted telephone. The next things I knew, is Edmond grabbed me around my throat and started to choke me. My mother grabbed him to make him turn me a loose. After everything cooled down, my mother called my grandfather (her father) to come get us to take us to safety. My mother and I left but she left my brothers.

 After a week or so, Shirley and Edmond reconciled their differences so Shirley could return to home. My grandfather told her that she could return but I could not go back into that environment; especially since I was not Edmond's biological child.

There had been signs prior that as Edmond's sons grew up I was an outcast. He had begun to make differences. I remember my last Christmas in the home with my mother. I asked for a bicycle. Instead of a new bicycle, they went to a junk yard and bought an old broken bike. My stepfather went to the local store and bought parts to make it like new. I remember it was large and spray painted green. The bike was so old and worn out, you couldn't peddle it up hill. It would only roll downhill. The bicycle chain was too old to do too much.

For me that was one of my distractions that could have been fatal. The series of events could have made me have bitterness in my heart for my stepfather. Might I add that that bitterness will kill. Bitterness is like cancer. It can slowly eat away at your happiness, self-worth, and cause death.

Let's talk about bitterness for a moment. "Hebrews 12:15. Looking diligently lest any man fail of the grace of God: lest any root of bitterness spring up trouble you, and thereby many be defiled." As it states in the bible, bitterness is a root. "A root is a source, or a bubbling fountain that is laying under the surface. A root's job is not to manifest on the surface, but to brew under the surface and fuel things that are on the surface. "If it had not been for God's hand on my life and him placing loving and caring family members in my inner circle I could have allowed the situation to take root. Thank God for his mercy. I thank GOD that he is a prayer answering GOD. I really realized a few years back that Jesus loves me and he answered my prayer.

I loved going to my grandparents' house. My brothers and I would spend the summer at their home while our parents worked. On Saturday after my step-dad and their dad got off work, he would drive 20 miles to our grandparents' home to bring us a few of our favorite foods and to visit us. I was very happy when I was at my grandparents' home. It just felt so right. Could it be because I was the first grandchild and the only baby?

My mother married very young; in fact, it was shortly after she graduated from high school. My mother's brother and sister were teenagers at home. So, I was the center of attention and surrounded with hugs and kisses; not to mention grandmothers' great cooking. I remember waiting anxiously for my grandfather to pick me up from my parent's home to take me to spend time with him and my grandmother. I would always get so anxious and excited; the time for him to pick me up could not come fast enough.

I remember when I was around 10 years old, my brothers and I had some type of argument so I called by grandmother and asked her to come get me. She said that she would come get me as soon as my grandfather got home from work. I went into my bedroom and began to pack all my clothes. I remember going to my dresser, pulling the drawer out of the dresser and just turning it upside down to dump it into my suitcase. I had so many clothes in the small suitcase that it wouldn't close even when I sat on it. When my grandparents arrived my grandmother asked "girl what are you doing with all these clothes". I replied that I called you to come get me. I am moving with you. My grandmother said, "I am only coming to get you for the weekend". I was sad and I remember saying at that point "Lord, I want to live with my grandparents". The Lord heard my prayer and he was mindful of me, even as a young child. Who would have thought that the fight my brothers and I had would open the door for my answered prayer? However, it was all in the plan of GOD.

The bible says in Proverbs 22:6 "Train up a child in the way he should go: and when he is old, he will not depart from it." The Lord allowed me to be raised in my grandparents' home so I would be required to go to Sunday school and church. I would watch my grandmother get on her knees at night and pray before she went to bed; and most memorable was listening to her sing a song called "Peace in the Valley and "Swing Low Sweet Chariot" while she was cooking. She instilled in me how to treat people. She would tell me to treat people how I want to be treated. I thought it was a scripture from the bible; well I guess in a sense it is. "St. Luke 6:31 says "And as ye would that men should do to you, do ye also likewise." KJV

The NIV says, "Do to others as you would have them do to you". So what the enemy meant for bad it was all part of the making for my future.

Ten months after I went to live with my grandparents permanently, my grandfather had a stroke that left him paralyzed on the right side. Thank goodness, my grandmother knew how to drive a car and take care of business; because now she had to take care of all the business and manage the finances. You see, this happened in the early 1960's. This was a time of segregation of the races and women were not allowed to learn to drive, in some instances, let alone handle business. God gave my grandmother an anointing for business. Thank goodness that the Lord is all-knowing and all seeing. He knew that my grandfather was going to have a stroke and that my grandmother would need someone to stay with him at home while she left to take care of business.

What possibly led to my grandfather having a stroke? Maybe he had a warning to change his life or lifestyle and refused. My love for my grandfather was immeasurable. He was the love of my life, he was the man that I knew for sure loved me, he was the man that would give me anything, and he was also the man that got drunk on the weekend and turned into a person I did not know. My grandfather worked all week; then on Friday evening on his way home from work, he would stop at the liquor store and purchase his bottle of gin. He would make several trips out to the garage to take a sip of his alcohol that he had hidden in the rafter. The more he drank the more aggressive he got towards my grandmother.

Growing up in a rural area, most men had a collection of firearms. The guns were used to hunt deer, squirrel, and rabbit. The guns were also used as protection because not all other nationalities viewed you as equal. Oftentimes when my grandfather drank, he would either chase my grandmother with the gun or point it at her. Regardless how he treated my grandmother, she continued to cook, clean, and treat him with respect. She just prayed continuously and sung her songs. The scripture tells us in Romans 12:20 KJV "Therefore if thine enemy hunger, feed him; if he thirsts, give him drink: for in so doing thou shalt heap coals of fire on his head."

After the doctor told my grandfather that, he had a stroke, for one year he did not try to walk or do anything. He just stayed in the bed. My grandmother had to bathe him, shave him, feed him and everything else that he could not do or he would not try to do for himself. The fingers on my grandfather's right hand drew up where he could not open his hand. My grandmother would say, "That is the hand that he would hold the gun". This situation was meant to be a fatal distraction but God used it as a tool to teach me the true meaning of the wedding vows "for better or worse and in sickness and in health". The Lord allowed me to witness a man, I truly loved, get overtaken by alcohol. My grandfather's behavior from overindulgence in alcohol caused me to set the first of many standards I did not want in a mate. I thank God that he honored that.

It was said that when my mother and her siblings were little, my grandfather moved to Arizona with another woman. He left his wife and his three children to fend for themselves and if it wasn't for my grandfather's father, who knows what they would have done because, my grandmother did not work. Maybe she didn't work because she had small children or maybe it was because women didn't work back then. My grandfather came from a rich family and he acted like some irresponsible men do. He spent his money on everyone but his wife and children.

"Romans 12:19 – Dearly beloved, avenge not yourselves, but rather give place unto wrath: for it is written, Vengeance is mine; I will repay, saith the Lord." KJV

My grandfather lived 11 years after he had the stroke. After about seven years, he got saved and gave his life to Christ. During the 11 years, I saw the Lord do a transformation in his life. He was at peace when he went home to be with the Lord.

CHAPTER 2

I WANT TO BE LIKE YOU

At the dawn of a new year, I could only imagine what was in store for me as I began to count down the months until my 16th birthday. As the days turned into months and as the seasons changed, I was suddenly approaching the end of my sophomore year in high school. This was an exciting time for me because I was preparing to embark on a summer vacation to remember while in California. Over the years, I had been blessed to have an uncle, my mother's brother, who loved me dearly. He made sure that I received a birthday gift and a Christmas gift each year. We called him Uncle Jaff.

Uncle Jaff left home right after high school to find a job so he could have a comfortable life and so he could provide for his younger sister, and his mother. Growing up was difficult for Jaff because of his father's my grandfathers alcoholism. Alcoholism caused my grandfather to neglect his family's basic needs. (I.e. food, clothing, etc.) Oftentimes they did not get Christmas gifts, like other children. Jaff purposed in his heart that when he graduated from high school, he was going to leave his home state, get a good job, and take care of himself. Jaff's first try at success took him to Minneapolis, Minnesota. He was unhappy there because of the extreme cold weather; therefore, he returned to his childhood home, which was in a much warmer climate. He became very discouraged because he was trying to get out of the horrible living conditions in his childhood home.

Jesus answers prayer –

My grandmother, Al's mother was a woman of prayer. She had to have a prayer life. She had a husband who was verbally abusive, an alcoholic, and he neglected his family. My grandmother always prayed for her children to have a better life. One day Al's mother had a surprise visit from a cousin she had not seen in many years. Her cousin's name was J. C. They began to play catch-up on all the family news. During her conversation with J.C., she mentioned that her son Al had graduated from high school and went to Minnesota for work but had to return because of the cold climate. J. C. mentioned that California was beautiful, warm, and that jobs were plentiful. Therefore, he offered to take Al back with him to California to help him get established. His mother told J.C. that she did not have any money to give Al but she wanted her son to have a chance at a better life. Nevertheless, Al moved to California and life was good.

As Al prospered, he sent for his baby sister after she graduated from high school to move to California. Her name was Louise. She was a very pretty girl with a very shy and naive nature. Maybe it was because she was raised in a sheltered environment, in spite of her alcoholic father. The change of location and environment caused her to prosper socially and emotionally. Louise began to explore her options as an adult. The move to California opened up a whole new realm of possibilities. Louise decided to further

her education by attending a local trade school. During her exploration of an education, she found something better. She met her Boaz. Her Boaz was known as Ryan.

One sunny day while Louis was lounging in the sun, she caught the attention of this short bow legged sleepy eyed gentleman. Ryan began to pursue Louise but she was not interested. She was very experienced in dating and she did not trust men, because of what she had seen her mother go through. Ryan was not use to rejection by women. He was use to women chasing after him. He was shocked and fascinated even more by this virtuous woman.

As the days progressed, she would slowly begin to trust Ryan's intentions. Ryan and Louise finally stopped the chasing and dating saga and married. It was a beautiful and happy time for them both. Ryan had married the woman of his dreams and Louise had finally married her soul mate.

Marriage is ordained by GOD.

In the bible, it does not specifically tell you step by step that marriage itself is going to be a challenge but it does talk about things like patience, trouble, struggle, pain. When the bible talks about issues in life, we have to realize that sometime marriage is where one or all of those things will surface in our lives. Louise was a true example of what the bible refers to in Proverbs 31.

Two years after Ryan and Louise's marriage, they were expecting their first child. This started out an exciting event but things begin to change. Louise's hormones were all over the place and it seemed as though Ryan was hormonal as well. Ryan was usually very good at keeping his temper under control but during this time, he was a ticking time bomb. As the pregnancy progressed, the bills began to mount up. Ryan's job was cutting hours and talking about a possible lay-off, which did not help the situation. It was frightening. Louise began to see a side of him that she did not know existed. He would get into fits of rage. He would throw furniture, punch walls, and yell. One day when she was trying to calm him down and reason with him, she was about seven months pregnant at the time. Ryan got so angry that he threw Louise down and began to choke her. When he came to himself, he realized that another spirit had taken over. At that moment, he began to weep and ask God to help him. Louise got up, wiped her tears, and began to pray with her husband. From that moment on, he began to change.

Ryan began to put Jesus in the center of their marriage. There were many instances where neither Ryan nor Louise knew what to do, but they made **Proverbs 3:6 KJV** their foundational scripture. **"In all thy ways acknowledge him, and he shall direct thy paths"**. Marriage is a challenge by itself and now they are adding another person, a new baby. They realized that if you serve the Lord, you must stand on His word. **"I can do all things through Christ which strengtheneth me. Philippians 4:13". KJV** They learned this early in their marriage. Later that year they welcomed their first son. Years later, they added three more children to their family.

May 30th marked the end of my sophomore year in high school and the beginning of my summer vacation in California. On Friday, June 1, I boarded a Greyhound bus for Los Angeles, California. The schedule stated that I would not arrive in Los Angeles until Sunday, June 3rd. You may ask why take a bus and not an airplane. You see, the cost of an airline ticket was very expensive in that day. Purchasing an airline ticket would have probably equaled the cost of an airline ticket to China in today's economy.

As I packed my clothes for my summer vacation, my grandmother instructed me on the basics of what to watch out for. I called it "How to Travel Alone – 101".

She said:

(1) Don't talk to strangers

(2) Listen attentively when the bus makes rest stops, (the announcer would call out bus numbers, door numbers, and destinations. Similar to what is done in the airport)

(3) Sit in the front of the bus near the bus driver,

(4) Don't let people see your secret place where you keep your money.

Grandmother had taken a little cloth bag and

pinned it to the inside of my bra with a safety pin. The cloth bag was all that remained from a previous bubble gum purchase. The bubble gum was called "Gold Nuggets". The gum was yellowish in color and was fashioned to replicate gold nuggets. Grandmother instructed me to go into the restroom stall whenever I needed to get money to make a purchase for food.

As the time on the clock approached 9:00, my heart began to beat faster in anticipation of the arrival of the Greyhound bus. At 9:00 a.m., the big silver and blue double decker bus arrived. The bus door opened. Out stepped a tall thin Caucasian gentleman dressed in the Greyhound bus driver uniform. The gentleman looked at my bus ticket, stamped it, and tagged my luggage. My grandmother told the bus driver that I was travelling alone to Los Angeles California. She went on to ask the bus driver to take care of me by keeping a watchful eye on me.

I boarded the bus and found my seat in the front, near the bus driver. As I left, my small town behind I was sad to leave my grandparents but I was also excited to see what adventure was waiting for me in California. The bus was very clean and comfortable. It was equipped with a restroom and very comfortable seating. The seat had a footrest and it reclined for sleeping or just relaxation. The air conditioner worked very well also. It was always very cold on the bus. It felt like it was 40 degrees inside. There were times when the cold temperature was a welcomed relief. I distinctly remember that the cold temperature felt great whenever we disembarked the bus in El Paso Texas and Flag Staff Arizona. The temperature in El Paso was 105 degrees and Flag Staff was at least 105 with a heat index of 110 degrees.

It was 5:00 a.m. Sunday, June 3; I finally made it to the bus station in Los Angeles California. I was a little disappointed because the bus station in Los Angeles didn't look much different from the one in Dallas, El Paso, Flag Staff, or Riverside. Well, at least all the bus stations were a building. My city didn't have a bus station at all. Our local Greyhound bus was a stop not an actual bus station. In fact, I walked out on to the sidewalk in front of our local drug store, now known as a pharmacy, to catch the bus to California. After looking around to access my environment to find a telephone I could use, I called my Uncle Al to let him know that I had arrived and was waiting for him to pick me up.

As minutes seemed like hours, Uncle Al finally arrived. I was filled with so much joy and excitement; I could hardly contain myself. The drive along the city streets was very quiet and calm. I guess that was because most people were still asleep. After all, it was only around 5:30 a.m. on a Sunday morning. Finally, we made our arrival to our destination, Uncle Al's apartment. As he opened the door and we entered the apartment, we were greeted by a lady. The lady introduced herself to me and stated that her name was Carron. I said hello, but in the back of mind, I wondered, "Who is this person"? I was in total shock to discover that my uncle had a female friend; especially a woman who I would later learn that I had to share my uncle with. All my life Uncle Al had been my best uncle in the world. He had been in my eyes, like Santa Claus and the Fairy God Mother. He was always concerned about every aspect of my life. (I.e. my grades, my attire, my manners, and anything else that concerned me.) I was used to being the center of attention. If I ever needed anything or just wanted to hear his voice, all I had to do was pick up the telephone and call. It was obvious that I had been living in some sort of dream world. It just never crossed my mind about my uncle dating. Maybe it was because all the family I knew was married. I mean me, myself had not even thought about not to mention or tried to go on a date.

Once I got past the shock, I slowly began to adjust with the idea of sharing my uncle. I must say that it was an adjustment because there were times I wanted to hang out with just my uncle; but more times, than not Carron was with us.

After I was settled in my room at Uncle Al's apartment, he took me to visit my Aunt Louise, Uncle Ryan and their children. They had a very nice home. The warmth I felt when I entered their home reminded me of my grandparent's home. You could just sense the love and peace. My Aunt Louise had prepared a nice meal to welcome me to California. The meal was amazing. Aunt Louise had prepared a beef roast, with homemade mashed potatoes, fresh English peas, homemade yeast rolls, strawberry kool-Aid to drink, and a homemade three-layer chocolate cake. Man oh man, it was a meal fit for a king, or should I say, just like my grandmother would have prepared. I was excited to see my cousins and I was excited about the possibility of spending time with them in their home. You see, prior to me coming to California, I would only see them at Christmas at our grandparent's house.

Well, after spending an afternoon with my aunt, uncle, and cousins; it was time for me and Uncle Al to head back to his place. As we arrived back at his apartment, it was time to go to bed and to see what the next day would hold. Before going to sleep, Uncle Al told me that I had to get up and be dressed by 7:30 a.m. on Monday morning. In my mind I'm thinking "why am I getting up early, I'm out of school for the summer, I'm in California, and most of all, I am on vacation". I decided not to worry about it but to go to sleep instead; tomorrow would take care of itself.

Early Monday morning I could see the sun peeking through the curtains in my room, when suddenly I heard an unfamiliar sound. What was that strange noise? Oh, it was a digital alarm clock. I had never heard one before. My alarm clock back home made a very loud and annoying ringing sound when it went off. I slowly crawled out of bed to get dress for my first day of my California adventure.

Uncle Al grabbed our lunch that he prepared the night before, and his car keys as he instructed me to head to the car. I could not help but wonder where we could be going this early in the day. So, instead of wondering I asked Uncle Al "where are we going"? His response was that he owned a dry cleaner and that he had to go open the store for his customers. Customers that needed their clothes dry-cleaned came by the store on their way to work. Oftentimes, customers would come to the Cleaners very early in the morning.

During our ride to work, my uncle began to explain to me his plans for me during my vacation with him. During my 15 years of life, I had been extremely blessed with family who loved me and made sure that I had everything I needed and several things I wanted. Some might say that I was spoiled. I call it blessed. Early in life I was taught to be respectful to all people, to be obedient, to not steal or lie, to serve the Lord, and to go to church. I never really had chores to do but I did help out around the house on occasions. Our home was small, I was the only child there, and both of my grandparents were home during the day.

Based off my lifestyle with my grandparents, Uncle Al wanted me to gain work experience by working with him at his business. Unknown to me, there was a discussion to plan my summer in California. This discussion was between Uncle Al and my grandparents. He commended my grandparents for all they had imparted into me, but he saw my potential and wanted to expose me to more. Uncle Al planned to teach me work ethics, purchase my clothes for my return to school in the fall, and to expose me to the cultural side of life.

Uncle Al took me to work with him at the dry cleaners Monday through Friday. On Sunday, we went to church. We did not go to just one denominational church. As part of my learning experience, he chose a different denomination church each Sunday. He wanted me to experience the different styles of worship. Also, part of my learning experience was to visit museums, art galleries, theatres, California beaches, and ethnic communities (i.e. China Town, Watts, Little Tijuana, etc.). I thank Uncle Al now for what he did. However, back then, I just wanted to hang out and be a teenager.

The bible says **"Train up a child in the way they should go; and when they are old they will not depart from it." Proverbs 22:6**

There were times that Uncle Al would let me spend Friday night with my Aunt Louise and Ryan. Those were my favorite times. I learned a lot about being a mother and wife. As I mentioned earlier, my parents divorced, I went to live with my grandparents; therefore, I did not have a real sense of what a family was supposed to look like.

My uncle Ryan worked outside the home and my Aunt Louise worked in the home. Her primary responsibility was to care for their children, their home, the finances, and her husband. I watched how my aunt spent time to nurture her children by training them, reading to them, discipline them, and loving them. Aunt Louise made sure her home was clean and welcoming. When Uncle Ryan returned home from a hard day at work and driving in the horrible California freeway traffic, Aunt Louise had a hot meal waiting for him. I watched in amazement each day Uncle Ryan's routine when he entered his home from work. First, he greeted Aunt Louise with a kiss, then he hugged each child individually, and then he took a shower. While he was in the shower and changing into fresh clothes, Aunt Louise was setting the table, with the help of the children, to prepare to sit down for dinner. The family always turned the television off and sat down together for dinner. Dinnertime was a special time for uninterrupted conversation. The conversations consisted of updates on all the daily activities of the wife, each child, and Champ. (The family dog)

Friday was a special day for the family. It was the day that my Uncle got paid, which meant Aunt Louise did not cook dinner because the family was eating out. When Uncle Ryan got home on Friday, his routine was the same with the exception of dinner. Friday night dinner was an exciting time because each child had a turn at selecting what and where the family would dine that night. The dinning selection was always some place simple like Taco Bell, Jack in the Box, Dairy Queen, or Pizza Hut. The most important thing was that the children got to take turns at decision-making and the family was together.

I learned so much from watching my aunt interact with her husband and children; that I made a decision to be like her when I got married and had a family. Years later, I thanked my aunt. I shared with her how my visits to her home during my summer in California had a positive impact.

It is so amazing that my Aunt Louise was doing exactly what the bible says in Titus 2:4. She didn't take me aside and say "this is what you should do" but she lived it daily. **"That they may teach the young women to be sober, to love their husbands, to love their children", Titus 2:4: KJV**

CHAPTER 3

HE'S NOT MY TYPE

All things must come to an end. As I prepared to end my summer in California and say good-bye to family for now, I could only imagine what my junior year in high school would be like. During the long bus ride home, I had plenty of time to reflect on all the things that had transpired. I could not really explain it; but I felt different and I looked different. During my vacation, I actually lost a few pounds and developed some curves. In my mind, I felt I was still my grandparent's baby but there were some feelings going on inwardly that I had not experienced before. What was really going on? Well, I am returning home, it was the end of August, which happens to be a little less than two weeks from my 16th birthday. What does that have to do with anything? Too, much thinking for a 15-year-old. I will just take a nap; after all, I am about an hour from my final destination, home.

Just as I get very comfortable, the bus driver announces that we have arrived at my hometown. As I prepare to embark from the bus, I see my grandmother waiting anxiously for me to step out the bus. Huge butterflies or bees are rumbling in my stomach. I ran towards her open arms and hug her tightly. I asked her to hurry and load my things into the car because I can't wait to see grandpa. I was so excited; I was talking so fast and saying so much that she asked me to slow down. I realized that it was a wonderful opportunity to have had the experiences in California but there was truly no place like home.

Once I unpacked my clothes and got settled, I called my best friend. I had not spoken to any of my friends all summer. Debbie was my best friend. She was one day older than I was. I spent countless hours at her house not to mention a few sleepovers as well. She told me that while I was away, her parents opened a little café on their property. The café was a safe place for teens and those who did not drink alcohol. The café only sold burgers, sodas, chips, and candy. There was a pool table and a jukebox. It was perfect for those of us under age. Her parents monitored the activities and the attendees. The jukebox was our source for music. We danced and just enjoyed hanging out with our friends there.

One day something strange happened. Debbie and I were inside the café with her older sister when two young men, whom I had seen at school, stopped by to check out the café. Debbie sister recognized them because they were in the class that had just graduated. The guys were actually freshman in college. One of the guys put some money in the jukebox so he could listen to one of his favorite songs. The other guy racked the balls so we could all play a game of pool. We all had a good time talking, dancing, and getting to know each other.

At the end of the evening, one of the guys asked me to go on a date with him to the movies. I was a shocked. I had never been on a date, I had never been asked to go on a date, I had never asked my grandparents if I could go on a date, and most importantly; what's a date? I told him I would have to let him know; so we exchanged phone numbers.

When the guys left, I asked my friends Debbie and her sister Diana; what do I do? For sure, the first thing I had to do was get permission. The thought of asking permission made me even more nervous. I had not so much as had a boyfriend before and now suddenly I 'm being asked on a date. Oh my! A date, with a college guy? If I went out, I had to take Debbie. She was my best friend and we were inseparable.

 Debbie and Diana helped me rehearse what to say to my grandparents when I asked the big question. I remember as if it was yesterday. My grandmother was in the kitchen cooking dinner. She had something boiling in a pot while she was preparing smother steak and gravy. I walked into the kitchen, pulled out a chair at the kitchen table, took a deep breath, and begin the process. I think it went something like this "grandmother…you know Miss Laura…. she said yes…well her son Sean asked me if he could take me to the movies. I thought I was going to pass out after I got it out and not to mention the huge boulder size knot in my stomach while I anxiously awaited her answer. She did not give me the answer right away. I think she was shocked that I asked such a question.

 Later that evening I heard my grandparents in a deep discussion behind closed doors. I could only imagine it was regarding my request to go to the movies. What she didn't know was, I was shocked as well. Nevertheless, my life was about to change.

 After about three or four hours, my grandmother said I could go to the movies with the following rules or stipulations. I could only double date, only date on the weekend, I could not go out every weekend, I could not go out on Sunday, she had to meet my date, and I had to be home by 12:00 midnight. Well, at least she said yes. Now I had to call Sean. During my conversation with Sean, I accepted his offer with the stipulations my grandmother had stated. Sean was okay with everything but finding a date for Debbie would be a challenge. If Sean wanted me to go out with him, he would find someone because we were a package deal.

Things worked out just fine. Sean found a friend to go out with Debbie. The four of us went to the movies. It was a little awkward but after all, I did not have previous dating experience. The movies ended with the two guys sitting in the front seat together, while Debbie and I sat in the back seat together. I was ok with that, because she was my friend and my security. Besides, I had never been alone with a guy.

Well, all good things have to come to an end. Sean and I had to drop Debbie at her home; then he had to take me home. I was a little nervous riding home late at night with a guy. Thankfully, he was a gentleman. He walked me to my door and said goodnight. Whew, he didn't try to kiss me or touch me. At that point I wasn't in a rush to date or go out. It wasn't a big deal.

Now that I had that experience behind me, I was excited about the start of a new school year; my junior year in high school.

The beginning of a new school year was always exciting. It was a time to see classmates whom you had not seen all summer. It was a time to catch on the latest fashion trends, what happened during the summer, and to see who was going to be in what class. This year had already started out different for me. I had gone on my first date. As my junior year progressed, it was filled with lots of class work, busy with band practices and band performances out of town, and travelling with the basketball team as a cheerleader.

One thing's for sure, my family made sure that I stayed focused on what was really important. My focus had to be family, church, and school. I was always reminded that I would have plenty of time for parties and playing after I completed my education. Maybe that is why I didn't have a boyfriend in high school. Don't get me wrong, I was very social. I was very active in extracurricular school activities, I was allowed to go to approved parties, and adult supervised activities.

The months past so fast that one-day it was September and the next thing I knew I was in the band practicing to perform at the high school graduation in May. Prior to May, I was reviewing brochures for colleges. After all, I had one more year to graduation from high school. Uncle Al suggested that I attend college in California and major in studies that would lead me to becoming a pharmacist since I was good in mathematics. My mother suggested that I attend a local university and major in music since I played the piano. During my research, I found a university in my home state that would allow high school students to enroll if they had 16 credits. It sounded quite interesting, so I applied and got accepted.

On May 31, my parents and I packed the car with items I would need for my time away at college. Later that evening, reality began to set in. As my mind began to wander, my first thoughts were; what in the world was I doing? My friends would be enjoying their summer, doing what teenagers do; especially before their senior year. Oh my god; there were so many emotions stirring on the inside. I was excited and I was nervous at the same time. After hours of tossing and turning, stomach churning with which felt like bees swarming inside, I finally fell asleep.

Early on the morning of June 1, I was awakened by smell of bacon coming from the kitchen. My grandmother was in the kitchen preparing breakfast. Grandmother wanted to make sure that I ate a healthy meal before I left for college. My grandmother was an amazing cook. She prepared all the meals in such a way, that whomever she feed, would feel the love and detail that went into every dish. I quickly got dressed and headed to breakfast. By the time, I finished breakfast, my mom and dad had arrived to pick me up to take me to college. I was sad to leave my grandparents but I knew that this was something I had to do. As I hugged and kissed my grandparents' goodbye, my grandmother prayed for safety on the highway and for a hedge of protection around me at school.

As we drove away, I reminisced that just the year prior I went to California. I could not even phantom what would be waiting for me at college. After a little over an hour, we arrived at the university in front of my dorm. The dormitory staff, who showed me to my room, welcomed my parents. As my father unloaded the car, which seemed like hours, but it was only about 15 minutes, I realized that this time I was surrounded by strangers, unlike the summer in California with family.

My mother helped me unpack and put my things in their proper place in my room. As we finished everything, I began to cry because I did not want her leave me. My mom began to fuss at me and told me to stop being silly. She did not have a soft side nor was she a nurturer. I have found that oftentimes, people portray to be hard or insensitive because they have been hurt. Maybe my mother had to be that way to cover the hurt that she had experienced as a child of an alcoholic and because of the destruction of her first marriage. Whatever the case, she was just that way.

As I dried my eyes, the door to my room opened. It was a young lady and her father. The young lady has been assigned to be my roommate. Her name was Sharon. My parents exited as I began to help Sharon and her father with her things. After Sharon got unpacked, we left to attend a welcome party for the new students. After the party was over, I went back to the dorm so that I could get ready for bed. The next day would be my first day of college.

The first day of college classes has finally arrived. As I wander around the campus trying to find the building where my two classes will be held, I suddenly realize that college does not even compare to high school. There are various nationalities of people who bring with them cultural diversities. As I enter my history class, I am in shock by my professor's teaching style. Mr. Green, my history teacher, gives each student a syllabus. The syllabus lists the chapters we need to read, the schedule of tests, and describes the grading scale. The syllabus list something related to grading called a "curve". I had never heard of a grading curve. And even worse, Mr. Green climbed up on his desk, sat down, crossed his legs "Indian style", and began to lecture. He did not have a book; therefore, I could not follow what he was talking about. I began to panic. What in the world, had I gotten myself in too? This was truly not like high school. I could not wait for the bell to ring, so I could exit that class. As soon as the bell rang, I gathered my belongings and headed for the Student Center.

As I entered the Student Center, a young lady who recognized me from the history class greeted me. She introduced herself and said that her name was Carol. We found an empty booth where we could sit and get acquainted. Carol and I each shared about our families, high schools, our education goals, and, of course, our thoughts on the history class. We had a pleasant time getting to know each other. After about 30 minutes, Carol's brother, who she introduced as Edward arrive to pick her up to take her home. Edward had completed his first year of college. He was also taking summers classes. We said our goodbye's until class the next day.

Summer school was different from attending fall and spring classes. Classes in the summer were Monday through Friday for five weeks. Classes in the fall and spring were either Monday, Wednesday, and Friday or Tuesday and Thursday for 18 weeks. Summer school was fast paced with lots of homework and tests. After all, the teachers had to cover in five weeks what teachers usually covered in 18 weeks.

Carol and I became good friends in a very short period of time. Maybe it was because she and I were both new college students or maybe because we were both from a sheltered environment. Whatever the case, we connected. The connection got even better because I had caught the attention of her brother Edward. One Friday when Edward came to pick up Carol, he asked me for my phone number. As I was writing my phone number on a piece of paper, I was screaming silently on the inside. Edward was tall, thin, and very handsome, not to mention a college man. I could not believe that he was interested in me.

Later that evening I received a phone call from Edward. Edward asked if he could take me to a movie; of course, I said yes. He mentioned that he and his brother shared a car. He stated he would call me back to confirm the day and time once he made sure the car was available. He went on to explain that his brother played in a band and that the band often had performances on the weekend. After the phone call ended, I felt like I was floating. Not to mention, I could not stop smiling. All I could think about was the idea of going out with Edward.

The day finally came for us to go out on our first date. All I could say was that it was magical. When Edward came to my dorm to pick me up, he was only allowed to go as far as the reception area. Young ladies who were freshman were housed in a protective environment. Gentleman were not allowed go anywhere near the sleeping area. Maybe the rule was in place because most of the young ladies had not lived away from home. When the receptionist called my room to let me know that I had a guest, my heart began to beat so fast that I thought it was going to jump out of my chest. Oh, my God, he was here; I could only imagine that this must have been how Cinderella felt. As I stepped out of the elevator on the first floor and started my walk toward the reception area, I could feel my legs get weak. As I turned the corner, Edward was standing there smiling as I walked toward him. He was dressed in tight starched jeans and a crisp polo shirt. As he reached out to greet me with a hug, I smelled the aromatic fragrance of his cologne. At one-point I thought, wow! He gently grabbed my hand as we walked out the door to get into his car. As he opened the car door for me, I realized the car he was driving was one of my favorites, a Ford Mustang GT. Cinderella may have had a glass carriage, mine was a Mustang.

The evening was more than I could have imagined. We went to dinner and a movie. Over dinner, we talked about sports, school, church, family, goals, music, and just about anything, we could think of. Edward was not only handsome; he was smart, intelligent, and a gentleman. From the first date, I liked him. I saw him briefly each day at school; after all, his sister Carol and I studied together every day. Carol commuted to school from home each day with Edward; therefore, he had to come get her when he got out of class. By the second date, I was in love. I had never been in love before. All I can say is, whew! Edward and I did not go out every weekend but when we did, each time it was like it was our first date.

I was so much in love that I forgot all about being homesick or wanting to go home on the weekend. I literally lived for the weekend and looked forward to going out with him. My mother often called to ask me if I wanted to go home, and I would say "no". So, she began to question me to try to find out what was going on. Me, not wanting to go home was totally out of character. I finally confessed that I had a boyfriend. My mother wanted to know who he was, where he lived, and who his family was. She or should I say my entire family was very protective and in some ways, snobbish. Before my next date with Edward, my mother had done her due diligence or should I say investigation on Edward's family. Surprisingly, Edward had not met the approval of my family but my mother actually knew and worked with his mother. I am not sure that was a good thing or bad thing. I think it was a bad idea. Edward's mother and my mother kept tabs on when we went out and what we did over the weekend.

The Fourth of July came and I was forced to go home for the holiday. All offices, including the cafeteria and dorms were closing on Friday afternoon to allow everyone to celebrate 4th of July Holiday. This was the first time I had been away from Edward outside of us meeting every other weekend.

My mom and dad made their arrival around 12:00 noon on that Friday to take me home for the weekend. It was great to go home to see my brothers and my grandparents, but in my heart, I could not wait to get back to school to see Edward.

I got up early Sunday morning, July 5 to start packing for my return to college. All I could think about was the thought of seeing Edward. I missed him so much. I know it sounds silly, because I was only gone two days. Maybe the reason I missed him so much was because our time alone together was only every other weekend. I said my goodbye's to my grandparents as we got in the car for my drive back to college.

I was so excited to finally make my arrival back on campus and to get settled back in my room. As I was relaxing in my room, I glanced out my window. Through the window, I spotted a car coming into the parking lot of the dorm. The color and the make of the car looked just like the car that Edward drove. The closer the car got to the dorm I realized that it was Edward. The first question that popped in my mind was "what is he doing here". Unfortunately for me, that question would soon be answered. As I looked out the window in disbelief, there was a woman in the car and it wasn't me. I was devastated. I could not believe that the person that I had given my all to had betrayed me. All I could imagine was that maybe he thought that I was still out of town. I did not realize then, but I do know now that the Lord's hand was on my life even back then. The Lord allowed me to see for myself what he was doing. I was determined to let him know that I saw him with my own eyes; therefore, he could not say that someone told me.

I decided to wait outside on the front steps of the dorm for Edward to return with his date. As I, waited outside with a few guys from a fraternity, we saw Edward's car turn into the parking lot. At some point, we realized that Edward saw me sitting there, because he turned around and left. I was determined to see Edward face to face with his date. I was prepared to wait outside past my curfew if necessary. All the females that lived in the dorm had a curfew. All females had to be in the dorm by 11:00 p.m. on a Sunday night. Finally, at 10:55 p.m. Edward turns into the parking again. This time he is forced to get out of the car and walk his date to the door. As he begins his walk up the sidewalk, I could tell that he and the female were both very nervous. I am sure they

were wondering what I had planned, especially since there were three or four guys with me. As they got in front of me, I just looked them straight in their eyes. I didn't blink and I made sure that I did not cry. I kept a straight face. However, on the inside, I was heartbroken.

After Edward got in his car and left; I went to my room and cried. It seemed like I cried an ocean of tears. I had just started the second summer session of school. I can truly say that summer session was the most difficult time I had experienced. I didn't want to go to class, I couldn't stop crying, I did not want to eat, and I could not wait for the summer to end. To make matters worse, the female that had gone out with Edward, came to my room to ask me if it was ok if she date Edward. That was the craziest thing I have ever heard, even to this day. She just needs to thank God that I was not into fighting or doing something crazy.

I made it to the end of the second summer session. I could not believe that in 10 weeks that I had fallen in love and got my heart broken. It was the wildest thing I have ever experienced. It was truly a different type of learning experience compared to my summer the year before in California. All I can say is that I was happy to be home with my grandparents.

I received my grades in the mail from the University for the Classes I had taken during the summer. My grades reflected that at 16 years old, I was disciplined enough to return to college in the fall and skip my senior year of high school. It was truly God, especially considering what had transpired with Edward.

As I prepared to return to college in the fall, I approached it with a different mindset.

I determined in my mind that:

(1) I was not going to fall in love

(2) I was not going to get my heart broken again

(3) I was not going to trust guys and

(4) I was going to focus on making good grades in my classes.

Well, it's time to pack up again and head off to the university. As we enter the college campus, there is a new level of energy and much larger number of students. The campus is bustling with parents driving U-Haul trailers, cars, and trucks stuffed to capacity with clothes, luggage, pillows, and stuffed animals. The fraternity buildings are proudly displaying the banners and the flags that distinctly differentiate the attributes of each organization.

I can't wait to get through the class registration process so I can begin my classes. I can truly say there are a larger number of guys at school this semester. The guys this semester appear to resemble a male lion on the prowl in search of their next victim. Discernment tells me to stay clear of these guys. The sophomore females warn those of us that are freshman to be careful; a confirmation of what I already discerned. I was sure that I would not be in the number, especially after what I had experienced weeks earlier in the summer.

Life was great for me. While I was home in August, I was informed that my Uncle Otis pastored a church in the same city as my university. I was determined to focus on school and to go visit my uncle's church. The only problem with trying to get to Uncle Otis's church was that I didn't have a car. There were several churches that sent their church vans to the campus to pick up students for church. Unfortunately, Uncle Otis' church did not offer transportation. I wasn't going let that stop me. I have always been very resourceful. I began to ask around campus about the church. The lord allowed me to meet a young man who actually attended my uncle's church. We had actually become good friends. Just friends, no string attached.

On Friday, September 11 was my 17th birthday. This was the first time that I had not been at home for my birthday. I never even thought to ask the Lord "what was he doing?" I was sad because I wasn't at my home celebrating. I knew not to ask my mom to come get me because she was very frugal or should I say stingy. My mother wanted me to stay at school and get an education. She was a no nonsense type of person. I could only imagine her saying "Gretchel, there will be other birthdays, or we will celebrate when you come home. I decided to make the best of living away from home. I purposed in my mind to get settled in and realize that the university and the city it was located in would be my new home for the next four years. I called my friend Randle to ask him if he would come to the dorm on Sunday morning to pick me up for church, and he said yes.

As I prepared my clothes for church, I began to get excited. I was excited to see Uncle Otis. He was a very special uncle. Uncle Otis got saved and gave his life to Jesus at the age of 17. He accepted his calling to preach the gospel at 17 also. He was very faithful to the Lord and he loved doing the work of a pastor. Uncle Otis loved his family. He always came to visit my grandmother. He would also come to encourage her during her trials with my grandfather's alcohol addiction.

Sunday morning finally came. I was excited about going to church. Instead of waiting to be called to come downstairs, I went downstairs to wait for Randle to pick me up. While I was waiting on Randle, a familiar face walked in. It was Alex. He worked in the college cafeteria. Alex loved to flirt with all the females. He worked in the area where you returned your food trays. Every time a female dropped off her tray, he would stick his head out through the opening for the trays and say something funny. He was quite a character. I proceeded to ask Alex, why was he at the dorm? He stated that he was there to pick up two young ladies for church. I told him that I was waiting on my ride for church but my ride was running late. A few minutes later Alex returned alone. When I asked him what happened, he said that the young ladies decided that they did not want to go to church that Sunday. He asked me if I wanted to ride to church with him since my ride was late. I accepted his offer because I hated being late for church.

As I approached the car with Alex, I noticed that someone whom, I did not know was in the driver's seat. Alex introduced me to the driver, which was his brother James. As we entered the church, I noticed that the music was quite different from what was played in my church back home. As I looked around the church, I noticed that the atmosphere was very different. First off, the person on the organ was playing without looking at a songbook or sheet music. There were instruments that I had not seen played in a church service. (Drums, electric guitar, tambourine, bass guitar, and triangle). The congregation was clapping their hands, tapping their feet, and some were even dancing with the beat of the music. It was totally different for me but the more I observed, the more I wanted to join in.

I was acknowledged as a visitor and to Uncle Otis' surprise; I was actually his great niece. I had a great time at church. After church, Alex's mother and sisters invited me to join them for dinner at their home. It was a welcomed change from cold sandwiches in the college cafeteria. Uncle Otis was invited to preach at a 4:00 p.m. service at another church in another city. Alex and his family invited me to ride with them. I gladly accepted their offer. It was a welcomed change from life in the dormitory.

While I we were still at Alex house I saw James watching me out of the corner of his eye. I was not interested him nor any other male because my pain was still too fresh from my break-up with

Edward. James was not my type. I usually liked the tall guys that all the ladies were trying to impress. Later that day James asked me for my phone number and if it was ok if he called me sometime. Me, being the polite person, I told him yes.

Later that week James called me. He was very pleasant to talk to. He was mature and he exhibited a lot of wisdom. We talked about how we were raised in two different economic backgrounds. James was the oldest of seven children, his parents divorced when he was 15, he had been the military, and his father was a womanizer and alcoholic. I was raised as the first grandchild of a wealthy oil family, parents divorced when I was a baby, raised by my grandparents, the oldest of my mother's four children. The one thing that we had in common was alcoholic fathers, divorced parents, strong family values, and strong religious background. I discovered that I really enjoyed talking to James. It was quite refreshing. He wasn't like your typical young college guys; only interested in getting physical. Not to mention, most of the college guys I knew weren't interesting nor could they hold a decent conversation.

James and I began to date. I found James to be very caring, respectful, polite, and a gentleman. I began to allow the Lord to take control of the relationship. It is amazing how GOD does things if we totally surrender to HIS will. In **Hebrews 13:4,** it speaks about "**Marriage is honorable in all** …." When I look back, it blows my mind and I still don't understand; all I know is that the word of the lord is true **"The steps of a good man are ordered by the LORD: and delighted in his way." Psalm 37:23**

I met James on September 13 had my engagement ring by September 30, and we were married three months later on the 19th of December that same year. Now that I look back, it was way too fast. But the LORD knew and he ordained it to be so. It was all in the LORD's plan for me to start college at 16 meet and marry my husband at 17.

CHAPTER 4

I CAN DO BAD ALL BY MYSELF

It was shortly after the marriage vows were exchanged and the return from the honeymoon that reality began to set in.

What was marriage supposed to be like? I was sure that the man of my dreams behavior would mirror that of all the soap operas I have so faithfully watched over the years. I was sure that my new husband was going to pick me up, carry me over the threshold, and shower me with bouquets of flowers each day. Boy was I in for the shock of my life.

The bible says in Genesis 2:24 "**Therefore shall a man leave his father and his mother, and shall cleave unto his wife; and they shall be one flesh**". **KJV**

Our first problem, we didn't leave-

We lived in a small town, which was the home to not one but two colleges. The second problem was that the availability of housing was limited to slim and none; mostly none. In spite of James efforts to find a house or an apartment, he was unsuccessful. He even looked within a 50-mile radius of the colleges, without any luck. So unfortunate for me or should I say us, we returned from our honeymoon without a place of our own. With that being said, we had to move into the house with his mother and his six siblings. The house had two bedrooms and one bathroom. This was quite a challenge for nine adults to maneuver getting dressed in the morning. For someone who grew up with their own bedroom and plenty of space, I had to ask the Lord what was I to learn from this. One thing for sure was in **I Thessalonians 5:18 "In everything give thanks, for this is the will of God in Christ Jesus concerning you". KJV** I learned that in spite of everything, we had a warm, safe, and clean place to sleep. Even though I cried almost every day, I tried to be thankful.

We tried to purchase a government-subsidized home. The mortgage company sent us a denial letter because our income exceeded the guidelines. In March of the following year, three months after we got married, we purchased a mobile home. Though we purchased the mobile home, we did not have a plot of land to set the home. As we began to pray and seek the Lord's face, we found a vacant lot in the city. We sought out the owner of the property. We finally located the owner of the lot so now we could ask him if he would rent us the space for our mobile home. Praise God! He said yes. We finally had a spot to put our home but it was difficult to set the mobile home because the ground was frozen. The frozen soil would not allow the plumber to dig the trench for the water line, the sewer line, and the gas line.

We were so desperate to move into our own space that we had the mobile home company move the mobile home anyway on to the lot. We prayed for weather to get above freezing long enough for the plumber to do what he needed to do. The Lord heard our prayers, the plumber was able to dig the trench, lay the lines, and connect everything. The water, sewer, and electricity passed inspection. We moved into our mobile home without any gas. I was so ready to move that I didn't care. We heated water for washing our face in a toaster oven. We went to James mother's house for bathing. Three days after we moved into our home the gas company came out and turned on gas. It was a happy day for sure.

Just as I began to enjoy my delayed alone time with my new husband; my mother-in-law challenges began.

You see, prior to me marrying James he was in the military. Upon enlisting in the military, James set up an allotment. An allotment, is when a person in the military can designate a portion of their pay to be given to someone, and in certain instances, the military matches the amount. The allotment is usually sent to the spouse but in James case, he authorized it to go to his mother. He understood the challenges his mother had as a single parent with six children at home. While he was in the military, he purchased a car. He left his car with his mother because he was deployed overseas. Life was good for his mother and his siblings; that is until he married me.

When we got married, his mother's allotment was gone and the vehicle she was driving went with us. Prior to us getting married, his mother tried to talk him out of it. Needless to say, I was not necessary a welcomed addition to their family.

Marriage, by itself is an adjustment. Let alone starting out the way we did.

Every day James mother needed him to come over for something. His mother needed him to come take her to the store or run an errand. Don't get me wrong, I didn't mind him helping his family but it was usually a six to eight-hour adventure. It just didn't make sense because we lived in a small town that only had two grocery stores and one store similar to Wal-Mart. Why would they need him every day and all day?

As time progressed, things got worse. James mother began to ask for money. It may not have been so bad if it was for groceries or a utility bill but it was to purchase a new outfit for one of his sisters for a church event. His sisters were very picky about where they purchased their clothes. They only wanted to wear clothes from the most expensive boutique in the city.

Money for us was tight. When we first got married, James was receiving a large check from the military for his injuries he sustained while he was deployed. A short time after we moved into our own home, the military doctors re-evaluated his medical condition. The doctors determined that he was now healed and able to work without restrictions. Our income was then cut to one-half of what he was previously making. Our bills were based on the previous salary. He and I both had to begin to seek employment. The challenge for me was difficult because I had never worked.

God was faithful. James and I both found employment. During that time James and I were trying to get our head above water, his mother was constantly calling asking for money. She may not have realized that she was manipulating, but each time James would tell her no she would try to put a guilt trip on him. She would say, "Well, I did the best for you that I could when you were growing up" or "I took care of you when you were little". It's a parent's responsibility to take care and provide for their children. It is not meant to be a tool to manipulate your children in later years.

Things between James and I got really bad. I was constantly complaining about him neglecting his responsibility to me. His responsibility was to take care of our home and me. The bible states in **Genesis 2:24 "Therefore shall a man leave his father and his mother, and shall cleave unto his wife; and they shall be one flesh". KJV** James grew up in church. He went to Sunday school every Sunday but somewhere along the way, this passage of scripture was not expressed enough; especially to the young married men and women.

James had gotten to a point that he would rather please his mother than me. He began to omit paying our bills to pay the bills at his mother's home. He not only paid her utility bills he paid her house payment as well. After the mobile home, we purchased a newly built home in the capital city. It was so beautiful. It had 3 bedrooms, 2 full baths, a living room, a den with a rock fireplace, and a two car carport. It was a far cry from the mobile home. It was in a brand new subdivision. It was five years after our marriage and shortly after our first son was born.

I noticed that we had started to get shut-off notices sometimes for the electricity. Then we started to get phone calls from the mortgage company. I began to question, where was the money going. To my surprise, James had started back paying his mother's bills and neglecting ours. Before long, we were so far behind in our bills that we had to move out of our home because it was going into foreclosure.

I had finally had enough. I decided to separate from James. There was an old blues song that said "I can do bad all by myself, I don't need any help to starve to death". I took my son and said "peace out". I knew that I deserved better. I loved him but it seemed that he loved his mother more.

After nine months of being separated from James, we decided that we wanted our marriage. The first thing that he promised was to live by Genesis 2:24. He also vowed to share our story and to teach other couples that their first responsibility is to each other. Not the children, not the parents, not the job, and not the church. Ministry starts at home then spreads abroad.

CHAPTER 5

FROM THE COCOON TO A BUTTERFLY

Merriam-Webster Learner's Dictionary defines a cocoon as "something that covers or protects a person or thing. ...to cover or protect (someone or something) completely ….."

As time passes, we have gone from minutes, to hours, to days, to weeks, to months, and to years. In that instance, we have gone from the protected environment, called our parent's home or in the case of the butterfly.

Scientist says there are four stages to become a butterfly. I say there are four spiritual stages to walking in purpose.

Let's look at the butterfly. The first stage of the butterfly is the egg. In our case, it is the seed that is planted in us as a child. The bible states in Proverbs 22:6 to "Train up a child in the way he should go: and when he is old, he will not depart from it." It was my parent's responsibility to teach me everything. In everything that means: they had to potty train, teach what things not to touch or not to do, how to treat people, and how to react or not react; the list goes on and on. Our spiritual training comes from the bible. We have to sit under a man or woman of God that is anointed and appointed to teach and train us in the things of God.

The second stage of the butterfly is the larva. The word larva in the dictionary is "any animal in an analogous immature form. I like what it says in the Merriam-Webster Dictionary "the early form of an animal (as a frog or sea urchin) that at birth or hatching is fundamentally unlike its parent and must metamorphose before assuming the adult characters." Merriam-Webster Dictionary defines metamorphose as "to change strikingly the appearance or character of; to be transformed". Once we give our life to Christ, we have to be transformed. It is a process. We have to study and meditate on the word. The bible says in Joshua 1:8 "This book of the law shall not depart from your mouth but you shall mediate on it day and night, so that you may be careful to do according to all that is written in it; for then you will make your way prosperous, and then you will have success". We have to grow in faith. Each time we take a step of faith in an area, our faith increases. Look at the story of David in I Samuel 17:34. When Saul told David that he was not able to go up against the giant Goliath, David begged to differ with him. David explained to King Saul that he had fought and killed a bear and a lion. Each faith experience is transforming us into the likeness of Christ.

 The third stage of the butterfly is the pupa. The pupa is when the butterfly is inside the cocoon; looking like it's resting but it is actually growing and gaining strength. Our pupa stage is when those trials and fiery darts come. In our pupa stage, we are praying, fasting, seeking God's face, and keeping our ear to the mouth of God. We are crying in our secret closet and making our petitions known to God. If we have been studying the word of God; then we know that:

(1) Ecclesiastes 1:9 "The thing that hath been, it is which shall be; and that which is done is that which shall be done: and there is no new thing under the sun";

(2) I Peter 5:8 "be sober, be vigilant; because your adversary the devil, as a roaring lion, walketh

about, seeking whom he may devour: "nothings new under the sun;

(3) I Thessalonians 5:17 "pray without ceasing"; and most importantly

(4) John 10:10 "The thief cometh not, but to steal, and to kill, and to destroy: (Jesus) I am come that they might have life and that they might have it more abundantly."

The fourth stage is the adult butterfly. I like to call it the mature or fully developed Christian. A fully developed Christian knows that Jesus is the same yesterday, today and forever more. If He did it before he will do it again. The bible says in Proverbs 3:5-6 "Trust in the Lord with all thin heart; and lean not unto thine own understanding. In all thy ways acknowledge him, and he shall direct thy paths." The key is we have to trust; even when we don't understand. The next thing is, we have to ask for direction. The Lord does not want us to fooled or running around like a chicken without a head.

Shortly after James and I rededicated our life to the Lord; all hell broke loose or should I say the bottom fell out. Prior to our re-dedication, we were living what some call the American dream. Both of us had good paying jobs, two children, a nice two-story home, and even a dog. We were on top of the world, so we thought. About 30 days after James re-dedication, the Lord called him into ministry. Call into ministry means that the Lord has tugged at your spirit or inner man to let you know that he wants you to teach or train his people in a great capacity. James said "yes" and at that point, we had an imaginary target on our backs. The devil had put a "hit" out on us.

I must say that nothing can happen unless the Lord allows it. We were going through the first stage of our butterfly experience. If you remember, the first stage is the teaching. We attended all the training our church had to offer. At the time, we did not know that we were being trained for what was about to happen. We just thought that we were being obedient to the Man of God, our leader. While we were in the first stage we were also in stage two. Stage 1 has many levels. Stage 2 is a dangerous stage for the butterfly. In stage 2, the butterfly is actually a caterpillar or larva. The caterpillar stage is a very vulnerable stage. Birds and other animals love to snack on caterpillars; therefore, the caterpillar needs to stay hidden until it is covered in the cocoon. As an immature Christian, we had to stay close to the vine: the church, the word of God, and our leaders. The trials could have made us vulnerable.

Approximately six months into our new lifestyle, my husband had to have a total knee replacement. He could no longer work, our income decreased by 75%, we had two children in high school, and our bills were escalating. All we could do was pray and stand on the Word of God. Suddenly we shifted from Stage 2 to Stage 3. As my family and I entered in Stage 3, the cocoon, the Lord gave us Psalm 91 for comfort and Proverbs 3:6 for instruction.

As we continued in the cocoon, we had numerous vehicles repossessed, our home went in foreclosure, and during one particular Christmas holiday, we could only scrape up $100.00 to purchase gifts for our children. We just kept standing on Psalm 91.

Psalm 91(KJV)

He that dwelleth in the secret place of the most High shall abide under the shadow of the Almighty. I will say of the LORD, He is my refuge and my fortress: my God; in him will I trust. Surely, he shall deliver thee from the snare of the fowler, and from the noisome pestilence. He shall cover thee with his feathers, and under his wings shalt thou trust: his truth shall be thy shield and buckler. Thou shalt not be afraid for the terror by night; nor for the arrow that flieth by day; Nor for the pestilence that walketh in darkness; nor for the destruction that wasteth at noonday. A thousand shall fall at thy side, and ten thousand at thy right hand; but it shall not come nigh thee. Only with thine eyes shalt thou behold and see the reward of the wicked. Because thou hast made the LORD, which is my refuge, even the highest, thy habitation; There shall no evil befall thee, neither shall any plague come nigh thy dwelling. For he shall give his angels charge over thee, to keep thee in all thy ways. They shall bear thee up in their hands, lest thou dash thy foot against a stone. Thou shalt tread upon the lion and adder: the young lion and the dragon shalt thou trample under feet. Because he hath set his love upon me, therefore will I deliver him: I will set him on high, because he hath known my name. He shall call upon me, and I will answer him: I will be with him in trouble; I will deliver him, honour him, with long life will I satisfy him and shew him my salvation.

When the butterfly is in the cocoon, he is strengthening his wings so that when he gets out; he can fly without restraints. During each portion of Stage 3, we were gaining strength. We knew with all our heart that our trials would not last always. Psalm 30:5 "For his anger endureth but a moment; in his favour is life: weeping may endure for a night, but joy cometh in the morning."

Two years later, we are finally in Stage 4. We truly came out with our hands up. The Lord is a restorer. The Lord increased our income; he blessed us with new luxury vehicles, and two brand new homes. Who wouldn't serve a God like that? His word is true. Isaiah 1:19-20 says, "If ye be willing and obedient, ye shall eat the good of the land." Also, Hebrews 11:6 says "But without faith it is impossible to please him: for he that cometh to God must believe that he is, and that he is a rewarder of them that diligently seek him."

Who wouldn't serve a GOD like that! It was a maturing process.

CHAPTER 6

THE SINS OF A FATHER

Earlier in this book, I shared briefly about my biological father. My father was raised by his mother and I am quite sure that he did not know who his father was. My father's mother passed away when I was about 13 years old. My fraternal grandmother had two sons by two different men. Back in that day, such behavior was frowned upon. By the time I got to actually meet my father, he had three daughters (including me). There are three of us with three different mothers. Do you see the pattern?

Some people do not believe in generational curses. I believe that there are generational curses and generational blessings. I also believe that when we accept Christ as our personal savior and become aware; then we have authority through the blood of Jesus Christ to cancel the curse.

I recognized early on that my husband and I had to break the generational curse of divorce and alcoholism. We were prepared to break the obvious curse of divorce and alcoholism; however, you do know that the enemy doesn't play fair. The one thing that I thought that we would not have to fight was infidelity.

If anyone would have told me that I was going to cheat on my husband, I would have told them they were crazy. I was so in love with my husband and I was also in love with being in love. I was what my friends called an incurable romantic. I watched Erica Cain on All My Children and I knew, that was how life was supposed to be. I wasn't supposed to suffer financial challenges. I was supposed to have a husband who catered to my every want and need. It was in that frame of mind where all the wrong seeds were planted.

Be careful who whisper in your ear. Friends would say, "You can do better than that" or "girl I wouldn't take that". The sneakiest thing that the enemy did was to tell me that "it was ok to have male friends and to go to lunch with them alone".

I was not prepared for what would happen down the road. I have always been a very friendly and sociable person. I always believed that I could be a good friend to men and women. In some cases, that is true but beware of the snares of the enemy. In Psalm 38:12 **"They also seek after my life lay snares for me: and they seek my hurt speak mischievous things, and imagine deceits all the day long." KJV**

I was being set up and did not realize it. The enemy knows what you like, how you like it, and knows what package to put it in. The enemy had me so blinded by what I didn't have financially that I couldn't see what I had.

I met this really nice single gentleman. He was tall, he had pretty white straight teeth, and not to mention a very athletic build. My husband was always working. He worked weekends, nights, and weird times of the day. When I was home, he was at work and vice versa. When I would mention that we needed to get away or go on a vacation, he would say, "I have bills to pay". If I asked him to go out to eat, he would say, "you go ahead without me". In the evenings when he worked, my friends asked me to go with them to happy hour. Oftentimes, I said no because I did not drink. But finally, I said yes. At first, it was a little awkward; but after a time or two, I got used to it. In fact, I began to look forward to it. I would laugh, dance, and share my problems with other men who had the same problem with their wives, so they said. After all, there was nothing going on at home. When my husband was home, he just sat at the computer and played solitaire. My husband did not have a clue that he and I were drifting farther and farther apart. The one thing that we had solid was love for our children and their well-being; so we thought. I realized that well-being is more than providing food, shelter, and clothing. Children can tell when something is not right. Children need interaction from both parents at the same time. Children need to spend time as a family. (I.e. bowling, movies, etc.)

I was so concerned about not drinking like my father and grandfather that I had opened the door to infidelity. I realized later that the one generational curse that my father had; had crept in unaware. Infidelity starts in the mind (a thought) before it becomes an action. What I initially experienced was "emotional infidelity".

It all starts with a conversation. Sometimes it starts over the internet, on your job, or at happy hour. Either way it is wrong. Emotional Infidelity has been defined as an affair of the heart. Emotional Infidelity is where you may be having secret conversations with a member of the opposite sex. You may share things with them that you should be sharing with a mate.

My feelings for my husband as a wife began to fade. I loved my husband but was not in love with him. B.B. King wrote a song titled "The Thrill Is Gone" and yes, it was gone. I loved my husband as the father of my children but that was it. I was determined to find the new man of my dreams that would help me take care of my children and me. Out of respect for my husband, I was planning on moving out and starting a new life. The idea of never getting a divorce went out the window.

As time grew", the grass began to look greener" on the other side of the fence". I began to contemplate and plan my departure. It included a plan to get my own apartment and start a new life. In my mind, what better place to find someone who would love and take care of me and my children than a military town. Surely, I could find the right someone among all the thousands of military men stationed or assigned there.

Within two weeks, I had found and leased an apartment. I began the process of moving things into my new place. The move-out was very easy because, remember, my husband worked different times. His work schedule caused him to be away from home at 14 nights per month.

All I can say is "but GOD"!

Thank goodness for the prophetic & what the word of God says in the bible **"For the gifts and calling of God are without repentance".** **Romans 11:29 KJV.** Several nights in a row, my husband began to have dreams about snakes. There were a large number of snakes in a ball. That was God's way of letting him know that something was going on. My husband's gift would always let him know if someone had been in our house. He would know if it was a male or female. When my husband's spirit was alerted, he would begin to pray against whatever it was.

My husband began to sense something was wrong. My husband is a very patient man; man, of wisdom, and discernment. He knew that eventually the truth would be revealed.

I began to ponder how I was going to tell him that I was moving out. Was I going to leave a note or would I have the strength and courage to tell him face to face? If I told him face to face, would he do something really crazy, like hit me? You see, my husband has a bad, bad temper. He was usually very good at controlling it but I have seen him mad a few times. My husband had never hit me, but people are not predictable, especially since I was taking his children out of his home.

The time finally came for the moment of truth. I decided to take easier of the two options; I left a letter on the nightstand in our bedroom on his side of the bed. After writing the letter, I got in my car and drove away to begin my new life; so, I thought. In the letter, I shared all my feelings that I had not been able to share in person. I also outlined my plans, which included a divorce. I waited a few days after my departure to contact my husband. I wanted to give him time to calm down. When I finally spoke to him by phone, he began to explain that he already knew because the Lord had already alerted him and the Lord had given him a dream. In the dream, he saw someone taking his children away from him. He could not see the face or gender or the person but he already knew, not to mention the dream about the snakes. I also mentioned that I had started the divorce paperwork.

Over a period of about two months, my husband and I had gotten to a point where we could at least be cordial. My husband tried to maintain relationship with our children. My husband expressed strongly that he did not like being a weekend parent only. His words fell on deaf ears. I was on a mission, to find Mr. Right, not just Mr. Right now.

It was a cool fall Friday night. My children had gone to spend the weekend with their father. I decided to get dressed up and head to the military base. As I approached the front gate of the military base, I asked the handsome soldier, who was guarding the entrance, for direction to the nightclub.

Following his directions carefully, I found the club. As I sat in my car planning how I was going to enter a club alone, my stomach began to churn and rumble. My heart began to beat a little faster and I could even feel a little tremble. Was I going to pass out, was I going to make a fool out of myself, what was I going to say, what where the people going to think? It seemed like my mind was racing one hundred miles a minute. I had never gone to a nightclub alone nor was I a drinker or a nightclub person. A voice in my right ear was saying, "Your mother is going to kill you if she finds out, what are you thinking, are you crazy?" A voice in my left ear was saying "You have to do this; your new man is here." So, after a tug of war with all the thoughts, I got out of the car and went into the nightclub.

As I entered the building, I walked carefully and tried to act like I knew what I was doing. With wobbly knees and shortness of breath, I saw an empty seat at the bar and headed there. In my head, I was saying, "look straight ahead, don't fall, just sit down, and catch your breath". Whew, I did it. Now what should I order, especially since I did not drink. I politely asked the bartender for suggestions. After he gave me some suggestions, I ended up ordering a coke with a cherry.

After about 30 minutes, a gentleman sat on the stool next to me. We introduce ourselves. He said his name was Kevin and he stated that he was from South Carolina. He was very pleasant to talk to and not to mention not bad to look at. After we exchanged phone numbers, I left to head home.

 The next day, which was Saturday afternoon, Kevin called. I was so excited. Kevin stated that he was out on his motorcycle and asked if he could stop by. I agreed to let him stop by because it was daytime and my children were not home. I had an enjoyable time getting to know more about Kevin. He mentioned that he was a divorced father of one daughter and that he had been stationed at the military base for three years. He also mentioned that he had been in the military for over ten years, he was planning to make the military a career, he had started a trucking business, and he loved God. Kevin went on to explain that he went to Nashville to visit his daughter every other weekend and to check on his trucking business. I was very impressed with Kevin, needless to say.

The following weekend, Kevin asked me out to dinner. I was a little nervous and a little anxious at the same time. When he arrived, he rang the doorbell and escorted me to his beautiful new BMW 735. He was such a gentlemen; he opened the car door for me. He remembered that I mentioned that I like Italian food so he took me to a new upscale Italian restaurant for dinner. Upon entering the restaurant, Kevin opened the door for me to walk in the restaurant first. He even pulled out my chair so I could be seated. I felt like a princess. No one and I mean no one had ever done those things before. They may seem like simple gestures, but for someone who had never experienced it, it was exciting. A short time after ordering our food, it arrived. As I was placing the napkin in my lap in preparation to dine on spaghetti, I noticed that Kevin bowed his head and blessed his food is a soft but confident voice.

You talk about impressed; I must say that I was. The more I talked with Kevin, the more I was convinced that he was the one. During our dinner conversation, Kevin mentioned that he was going to have to go to Nashville and purchase a vehicle for his ex-wife. In my mind, I thought was a bit much, but after hearing Kevin's logic, it made sense. He stated that he did not want his ex-wife to have to take his daughter out in the cold to wait at a bus stop. He said, "If his ex-wife was walking, so was his daughter". And he didn't want that, especially since he had the finances to purchase a vehicle. The other factor that made me think that Kevin was the one was his respect for my children, my home, and me. He told me that he would not come to my apartment if my children were there. For him, it was a respect thing.

I was so, so, so excited. Kevin was the one. I could see a future with him. We had great conversation and great times together. He took me as his date to a very formal event for the military; that meant I was really a special person. I even got to ride with him on his Honda Gold Wing Motorcycle. I was having a ball, life was good.

Then suddenly-

I remember as if it was yesterday. It was in mid-October, on a cool Monday evening when I received a call from Kevin. Kevin asked if he could stop by my apartment for a few minutes. He went on to say that, he needed to talk to me about a situation. I knew that it had to be important because he never came to my apartment when my children were there. Over the weekend, Kevin had gone to Nashville to visit his daughter. The week prior, he was on duty for 16 hours each day for five days. My mind began to ponder and speculate as to what he wanted to talk about. Surely, he wasn't going to reconcile with his ex-wife. What on earth could it be? Oh well, I would soon find out.

My heart began to beat a little faster and I became a little anxious. It was a combination of being excited to see him and the anticipation of finding out what he wanted to talk about.

Finally, the doorbell rang. As I calculated my steps toward the door, my face began to light up. I opened the door and there he stood. He had a big smile on his face and the aroma of his cologne was mesmerizing. In my mind, all I could say was my, my, my.

After greeting him with a big hug, I lead him to the sofa to have a seat. As we sat on the sofa, we played catch-up on the week's prior events as well as the weekend. Then he dropped the bombshell. He had been selected for a special assignment in Korea. The assignment was for three years and he was scheduled to leave in seven days. He went on to say, that he really cared for me but we were not ready for any type of commitment and he would not dare ask me to wait three years for him. Also, the assignment was one that did not allow families to accompany the servicemen. I was devastated. Kevin was the perfect man; I thought he could've been a husband to me and a father to my children.

As I walked Kevin to the door and said goodbye, I began to question God. I really did not understand why he would dissolve this relationship. After several days of walking through the disappointment, I began to just focus on work and taking care of my children.

No sooner than I had decided to move on with my life again, my car broke down. My car actually broke down on the interstate on my way to a church service. I asked the Lord, now what's really going on. I said, "Lord you know I don't have any extra money", Lord what am I going to do? The diagnosis from the mechanic said that I needed a head gasket. I wasn't sure, what that was I just knew the cost to repair the car was more than I had in my bank account. My only option was to catch a ride with a guy who worked for the same company as me. The only problem was that he had to be at work at 4:30 a.m. and I did not have to be at work until 8:00 a.m. Not to mention, that meant that I would have to leave my children alone in the apartment until time for school. The good thing was that their school was within walking distance and they walk with the other kids to school. I prayed and made the decision to go into work very early.

I really hated to tell my soon-to-be ex-husband about my situation. After all, I was trying to move on with my life, be an independent woman, and find Mr. Right. I had no other choice than to share with him my dilemma. At first, he was angry and accused me of trying to ruin his social life. I was just as upset as he was. I told him that "I didn't ask you to come and stay at my house; I don't need you any way. I am doing just fine."

In all of that, God had a plan. My husband would come to my apartment to stay with the children while I left for work very early in the morning. After about two weeks, the tension between us began to lessen. During our separation, my husband had moved on with his life also. He had begun to date several women simultaneously. During his stay at my apartment, he voiced that his women were upset that he was at his ex-wife's apartment. Me, being the stubborn person I am, told him that he was free to go; however, he didn't leave.

As time progressed, we began to talk. This was the first time that we actually shared our hearts with each other. We shared the good, bad, and the ugly. Men of his era were taught to be strong, to not show their emotions, and to guard their heart or as some like to call it that inner most private part of your being. His heart softens and he agreed to help me purchase another vehicle. My husband confessed that he had always told God that when he got married it would be for life and one-time. He also said that no matter what, he would not get a divorce. That is why I had to file for divorce; he was not going to do that.

I thank God that He honors prayers and the prayers of people praying for us. I thank God for my husband, my best friend, my encourager, my ride or die, the father of my children, and God's set man. Now we can talk about anything. We work together and not against each other. When people look at us and see our glow, we just say "It's God", we have a story to tell that would blow your mind".

I thank the Lord for cancelling the many distractions in my life that was meant to be fatal. I thank the Lord for praying parents and God's hand on my marriage. He has allowed us to weather many storms. We truly don't look like what we have been through. God allowed us to go through each situation and come out with tools. We have some tools that we can use to help other people. We are now on the other side of 40+ years of marriage. We give all the glory and honor to God!

CHAPTER 7

PURPOSE DEFINED

Psalm 37:23 "The steps of a good man are ordered by the Lord: and delighted in his way." KJV

When GOD created us, he not only had a plan but a purpose. The person he assigned it to can only fulfill the purpose that GOD has in mind. The best example I can give is an automobile key. The Nissan Armada key was not designed to work in the Nissan Maxima. Both vehicles were produced by Nissan but each vehicle was designed with a different purpose in mind. The same is true for us.

From the moment, we are born we are molded or influenced by our family, friends, society, and as I like to call it "life". Day after day, we go about our day doing our rituals or routines until that spiritual awakening. Sometimes that awakening comes through a song, a spoken word, a visual observation, a dream, or a random thought. The day of our awakening or the day, we come into conscientiousness of who we are and who He has designed us to be is truly a life-changing event. From that point, we are charged with discovering how we can accomplish what GOD has ordained for us. We must seek the LORD for direction and instruction.

Proverbs 3:6 "In all your ways know and acknowledge and recognize Him, And He will make your paths straight and smooth [removing obstacles that block your way] Amplified Bible

Proverbs 3:6 "In all thy ways acknowledge him, And he will direct thy paths." American Standard Version

As we begin the process of trying to walk out the purpose and plan of the God, we will stumble and sometimes fall; but we have to get back up and keep pressing toward the mark (our goal).

Don't get discouraged during the process. It has been said that most inventors failed several times before their invention was created. There have also been numerous successful businessmen that went bankrupt before they finally succeeded. The infamous Tyler Perry was sleeping in his car when he gave it one last shot to submit his first "Madea" play; and now the rest is history for him.

 God is not a respecter of persons. If he did it for others, surely he will do it for you. If He said it, He will bring it to pass. We just have to do our part.

CONCLUSION

I thank the Lord for not allowing my distractions to be fatal. I thank Him for counting me worthy to walk through many the trials.

There are people in the bible that had distractions which were meant to be fatal, but God said not so! God had a plan. Some were talked about, despised, betrayed, didn't speak well, and looked down upon. They sound a lot like many of us. In case you don't remember, I will share with you a few of them.

The Lord chose Rahab, a prostitute, who was a believer in God, to protect and hide two Israelites from the king of Jericho's death wish. God chose Moses, who stuttered, to be deliverer for his people. Moses had a hit out on him before he was born. The king had ordered that all males under the age of two years old to be killed. Moses was found by the king's daughter and raised as her son. Then there is Joseph who was despised by his brothers who sold him into slavery. Joseph had to give food to his brothers during a famine. And the list goes on. There are so many others spoken of in scripture.

Thank you LORD for choosing us! The bible says that we will suffer persecution and that we will suffer afflictions. The good news is that the battle is not ours it is the LORD's. The challenges of this world may distract us but the word of GOD tells us not to look to the left or the right but to focus and keep our eyes on the LORD. Weeping may endure for a night but joy comes in the morning.

I thank GOD for the night and the morning. Thank you for walking us through the distractions but most of all thank you for not allowing us to be destroyed!

Notes

References:

King James Bible

Amplified Bible

American Standard Version

Merriam-Webster dictionary

Print Layout/ Interior- by Corliss Y. Meredith

Book cover and author's page designed, created, and illustrated by:

Melissa Casole

http://www.thirdidsignz.com

Stay connected with Apostle Gretchel Dixon by:

Emailing her@ gdm.heart2heart@gmail.com

or connect with her on

Social Media

About the Author...

Apostle Gretchel and her husband, Apostle James, are the founders of Life Changing Ministries International of Austin, Texas and Empowerment Faith Christian Center.

Gretchel Hamilton Dixon was born and raised in southern Arkansas. At the age of 18 Gretchel realized that she had a call on her life to preach the gospel. She was told that women were not called to preach but they were called to be a missionary. She never doubted for a minute what God had spoken to her. She held on to that word until the set time for the manifestation.

In 1992 Gretchel, her husband and sons joined Trumpet in Zion International Interdenominational Ministries in Little Rock, Arkansas which is now Awareness Center International under the leadership of Apostle Lawrence E. Braggs. During her time at Trumpet in Zion God begin to stir up the gifts and began to manifest what He had spoken in her life several years before. Gretchel openly acknowledged her call to ministry and hence began her training. At the completion of her training she became a licensed minister. During her time at Trumpet in Zion, Heart to Heart Women's Ministry was birth.

On October 2, 2011 Gretchel returned to Little Rock to participate in an Affirmation Service. Chief Apostle Lawrence E. Braggs officially affirmed Gretchel as an Apostle by the laying on of hands, anointing with oil, and prophetically speaking into her life.

Apostle Gretchel has a heart for God's people. She ministers under the unction of the Holy Ghost in the gift of healing, teacher anointing, preaching anointing, and the prophetic.

She has a Bachelor of Science in Organizational Management and a Master in Business Administration. She is mentor, life coach, encourager and a motivator. Apostle Gretchel is a wife, mother of two adult sons and the grandmother of three granddaughters (two of which are twins).

She is a well-known and much sought after speaker and teacher. She speaks life!

www.ingramcontent.com/pod-product-compliance
Lightning Source LLC
LaVergne TN
LVHW051808080426
835513LV00017B/1866